TRUCE

HEALING YOUR HEART
AFTER DISAPPOINTMENT

TRUCE

HEALING YOUR HEART
AFTER DISAPPOINTMENT

by

ROB HILL SR.

**Spirit Filled Creations
Publishing**

Spirit Filled Creations Publishing
3509 Kids Court
Chesapeake, Virginia 23323-1262
Email: spiritfilledcreations7@gmail.com

Manufactured in the United States of America

10 9 8 7 6 5 4 3 2 1
ISBN 978-0-9653696-2-6

TABLE OF CONTENTS

TABLE OF CONTENTS

Part Four: CLARITY 76

Part Five: EVOLUTION 97

Introduction

There are many things men and women can disagree about, but the one thing we can't argue is that for each of us, life happens. Growth is about appreciating when life is good, while also learning to deal with things that are beyond our control. These experiences either break us or shape us into stronger individuals.

There is a beautiful design for harmony between men and women. **Truce** is an opportunity to discover love's true potential. Centuries of "the battle of the sexes" have left us with an improper, and at times, unhealthy understanding of one another. When our relationships don't go the way we want them to, we begin to feel like something is wrong with us. Men and women need time... to grow, to learn, to heal, and to reconsider the ways we attempt to love each other. **Truce** is a guide for us to meet all disappointments with faith in ourselves and the future.

Love happens in its own timing, and none of us can control that clock. Sharing the lessons once we've learned from our experiences with love is key to our own growth and the growth of others. I built a career as an author and speaker by sharing the truth as I found it. Through words, I share how I've learned to love myself first, then others.

I know that things happen and it's hard to weather the pain of a divorce, break up, or sickness. Still, we are never cheated out of the opportunities that are meant for us. In most cases, our experiences teach us what we need to grow as people, and there are valuable lessons in everything we experience. And through it all, we must choose to get better.

It took me some time, but I finally realized that romantic relationships are not where my love stops, and they won't always be the peak of yours either. Love is not limited in that way. There is more to our fulfillment in life than finding "the one." We form relationships to help us enhance our lives. Finding a partner through thick and thin is a gift. But I've learned that love alone does not make growing together easy or automatic. There are no guarantees in love. We get what we work for, and we grow as we develop the discernment to choose a partner who is willing to work with us. We have to stop overthinking. When we can stop overanalyzing love, then we will finally experience it.

It's hard, but when life is throwing blows don't waste time pointing fingers and placing blame. Protecting the heart is less about finding faults and more about processing pain. Emotional duress can ruin our relationships if we are unable to be introspective. We all have to deal with making mistakes under difficult circumstances. It's about accountability, not judgment. Too many of us judge people at all levels—friends, family, and lovers—tougher than we judge ourselves.

But why do we judge at all? For loving? For losing our balance? For not being everybody's perfect? It's natural for people to battle with pride and choices on occasion. However, when it's real love, the good partners aren't busy judging our steps. Those with real love in their hearts are more focused on helping us stay balanced on our journey together.

Forgiveness is a process. When we are hurting, we have to speak out about it to let it go. Hearing our own voice when we are processing is quite therapeutic. There is nothing wrong with being honest about feeling overwhelmed and undervalued. We've all felt the resentment that follows rejection and regret. But lasting love only happens for those who forgive because it sets them free. They can stay focused and get to the calm of life's storms.

An old proverb says, "Those who love like rain, soothe every fire." Dealing with painful memories is a challenge, but the result is greater focus and a strong heart.

The opposite of love is fear. Though many may suggest that hate is the opposite of love, fear is actually more accurate. Love softens people, while fear hardens them. Love opens the universe; whereas, fear shuts people out.

Fear comes in different forms. We can be afraid of failure, rejection, change, loss of power, and even our own personal growth. Think for a moment, who are you willing to become in order to have a life without fear controlling you?

Can you still love and accept yourself each day, even if you made some mistakes?

If you feel you got it wrong a lot, can you still encourage yourself?

Can you feel whole, knowing and trusting in all that you are?

We cannot be afraid to search within and trust what we learn about ourselves. The answers to all our questions come through understanding, not bitterness. We cannot stay stuck in despair because our feelings got hurt and things didn't go our way. The reality is, pain is a signal informing us that things are changing; it introduces us to our strength. Though fear tries to reject it, when we accept love, it reveals the greatness inside of us.

Many of us do the best work for our relationships while we are not in them. We develop new habits, perspectives, and boundaries, with hopes of not repeating the past.

A major thing to learn while single is that everything isn't for everyone. Some people find love in an instant, but for many of us, there are a few tests to conquer. To know that past relationships and mistakes do not mean that we cannot become a healed, loving person is comforting. Yes, people are going to get hurt along the way; but knowing we can heal can give us strength.

I wish there was an elevator to ride that could help us grow without the presence of pain, but I haven't found that "going up" button yet. Instead, I have found a **Truce**. A plan for peace. I know we can use pain, disappointment, and love as our catalyst to evolve to a truer self. We can make sense of our story until it's empowering, and we can have a clear vision of who we are.

We can use our past experiences to encourage us, and we can let our mistakes inspire us to continue to grow, transform, and love. **It's time for a TRUCE.**

.

TRUCE
Part One:
TRUST

1. What is Trust?

E ach of us has our unique understanding of what trust means, based on our own life experiences. We define trust in a very personal way. My definition of trust is having a belief in something or someone. It's knowing the person or thing is reliable, strong, and true.

Trust is not always easy to establish, but it is essential in every relationship that matters to us. I continue to learn the importance of trust through times of triumph and of disappointment. To give you an example, I trusted the gifts and abilities that I had within me when I decided to leave a successful career in the Navy to become a full-time father, entrepreneur, and author. The triumph from that decision gave me more flexibility in my schedule. I never missed a field trip with my son, and I established a fulfilling career path. Through the latter, I was able to create more avenues for income than I would have ever imagined.

This process of learning to trust also includes times of unforeseen disappointment, especially when it comes from those we love. I have faced betrayal from people I thought had my best interest at heart. I had to let go of them, even though I continue to care about how they are doing. Over time, these and other occurrences have had a profound impact on my ability to trust myself when it came to choosing a partner and trusting people in my day-to-day experiences.

There are different levels of trust, depending on the nature of the relationship. Early on, we learn trust through our parents, immediate family members, people we choose as friends and lovers, and even the people we work with. But it really all begins when we trust ourselves. When we don't trust our own confidence, we set ourselves up for an exhausting challenge to build stable relationships. It is human nature to want relationships that make it possible to trust without the fear of disappointment.

Yet there are times that it is lonely standing on the fence in life, unable to trust the one voice you should: the one inside of your head.

There is a part of you that knows exactly what trust should feel like. It isn't the part that remembers the relationships that didn't work out. It is the part that was holding you together when you thought it was time for everything to fall apart.

Trust also requires a level of personal security and integrity. It asks that you be sure of yourself before needing assurance from someone else. Trust is not the pathway to defeat, it only feels like that when our expectations exceed our knowledge and experience. Trust is the gateway to healthy relationships. It is the path you take when you want to stand on something firm and real. Without trust, the focus is on that physical and emotional feeling of spontaneous love. It feels great when you are on a "love high," but it will not sustain a healthy day-to-day relationship. Though irrefutable love can stand the test of time, steady relationships do not last without first a foundation of trust.

Throughout my personal journey, my willingness to love has evolved. My understanding of what it is to trust had to expand. My goal was to stretch my mind and thoughts beyond the confinement of the pain I held in my heart. For me, learning to trust was the first step to healing after a devastating disappointment. I knew then that before I felt confident enough to affirm another human being, I first had to seek within and face the root of what caused my pain.

The Root of Trust Issues

The root of trust issues does not come from rushing to find every minute problem with a person's character. Our most tangled issues with trust come when we have moral conflicts with our own behavior. Facing the root of where we are in our issues with trust allows us to develop the strength needed to break ties. The enormous weight of guilt, shame, and mistakes can lift when we finally decide to adjust our connections with those who have hurt us. Knowing how to get to the seeds and depths of our pain is an important part of building a positive flow of trust. Without knowing, we wander aimlessly, repeating our own history.

Below the depths of your pain is your living soul. If you bring hate, spite, and negativity there, you are poisoning the very place you claim to be defending. Hurtful memories, rejection, and feelings of doubt do not live in your soul. These emotions swirl around in your mind. When you take charge by changing your thoughts, the negative stuff will fall away and make room for you to grow. Keeping an open mind is vital. Sometimes when you think the rain is coming to ruin what you have planted, it's actually there to help grow your garden. What seeds are you planting?

When your partner cheated, did it cause you to question your self-worth?

Was the infidelity connected to the pain you watched your mother experience when you were a child?

TRUCE — Healing Your Heart After Disappointment

Spending your life in fear has taught you to be the first to leave before everything falls apart. Lack of trust usually stems from a place of fear, discovered or developed through pain.

But now you are ready to end the fear because being scared has not served you in any way. Instead, courage develops through the trials, and your experiences mold you for your purpose in life. From here on out, having trust depends on your ability to bounce back from disappointment and everything that was trying to hold you down in the first place. Fear doesn't belong to you, and it is time to let it go. I need to repeat that. Fear does not belong to you, and it is time to let it go.

What are you afraid to release? Clinging to old things is going to get in your new way. Where do you see an opportunity for freedom from the negative energy, pain, and resentment now residing in your heart?

Are you taking time to heal, to learn from your mistakes and choices? Or have you been blaming others for things that are yours to control? What about the things and people you can't change - why are you still holding on and giving them power?

6

Life experiences – every one of them – are opportunities for growth and healing. Life will place you in many different positions, some favorable, and some will feel unfair, and at times, putting forth effort seems pointless.

But there is a reason why the things that hurt you cut so deep that they make you hold back from opportunity and relationships. It is not because you are weak or because anything is wrong with you. More than likely it is because your thoughts are more focused on what can go wrong than on what you deserve and what can go right. The cuts, like your heart, will heal only when you let go of the past and trust yourself.

Disappointment and fear may cause a storm inside of you but as you know, the calmest place of any storm is at the center. Getting to your center and finding your core is a personal journey everyone must take for themselves. The path is designed for personal care, positive affirmations, exercise, and a nutritious diet for a healthy body and mind. Sticking to these roots of growth can keep you from getting lost in life's storms. Your soul is ready to blossom in every season of the year.

It is time for a secure relationship with trust and a healthy love of yourself. Look within and make the decision to clean out the things that don't belong anymore. You are not neglecting your heart, you are protecting it.

Your growth will need you to make changes. It may mean losing some of the people you thought would stay in your life. It may feel like you are missing things you need. But shift your thinking toward all that you can gain from trusting the process.

Choose now to move forward. You are ready for something better. And that means you will lose the things and relationships that are broken. When you change, and you're open to a new perspective, you begin to gain wisdom. Only then will you be ready to deal with disappointment.

Choosing to think, feel, and grow toward fulfillment: now that's a good life!

You won't outgrow anyone who's meant to be there beside you. This is a fact of life that you can count on.

2. Trust Yourself: The Personal Choice

N o one is exempt: we all must make a personal choice to be whole. This decision, while agreed upon in an instant, will take a lifetime of commitment to see it through. To be whole means to heal, and to heal means to establish a rock-solid balance. This balance is the healthy development of our physical, intellectual, and spiritual nature. The hard times have a way of making life feel stifling. We must resist the tendency to let our temporary moods get in the way of our goals. If anger takes over and blinds you in a relationship, make a choice to deal with it. If financial problems start to affect your confidence in people you care about, choose to help. Life's blows can knock anyone off balance, and these imbalances always affect our emotional well-being.

But your personal choice to be whole shouldn't be an emotional one. Your moods may go high and low and your feelings may confuse you, but this decision needs to be clear. You must make this choice for you and you only. This process of healing is all for you. You do not need permission from anyone else to be whole.

The personal choice is the beginning of acceptance; it is choosing a complete way of life. It is taking off the mask you use to hide the bad days. It is identifying any brokenness that needs repair. And it is deciding that every feeling of lack is worth acknowledgment. The personal choice is knowing that fulfillment is possible in your life. The process may begin with fear, and you may hear a part of yourself say, "I'm not ready for this, I'm not ready to trust." And then it happens: doubt, stress, worry, and uncertainty. You feel these things because you know this isn't something to take lightly. You recognize the signs.

Healing from the things that hurt us is not easy, yet with love, it is something we feel empowered to do without limits. Now is the time to feel limitless. Rejoice in the fact that you can still grow even when you don't feel like you're ready to change.

You are not alone in making your personal choice to be whole. Many like you make choices, hoping to improve life as they know it. Some choose with a desire to be more in tune with God. They are looking for clarity, purpose, and meaning in their lives. Others decide to be whole because they have felt broken for far too long. They see the process as a way to improve themselves and the people around them. Becoming whole is less about what has happened to you in life and more about what you want to happen next for you in life. You have a wonderful chance to love without the presence of fear. You are alive to know more about success than suffering. You may feel alone, but you are not alone. Trusting yourself and being willing to change are the first steps toward a better life.

Trust Is A Two-Way Street

Trust is a two-way street by design. It requires that you give and I give: you accept, and I accept. We are offering each other our understanding as we deal with the potholes in life and accept the accidents that happen when we didn't see them coming. We are giving room for growth and accepting days of struggle. We are providing support when things feel delayed. And we are taking responsibility when there are things we can change. Giving and accepting are important in relationships. They don't make mistakes something to be hidden.

The openness allows being "wrong" – something both partners can learn from. But when a person refuses to give you respect or accept responsibility for how their actions have affected you, the flow of trust on this two-way street turns into a dead end. When we're hurt, we don't want to let people in as we would when we're feeling steady. We do things that sabotage our ability to make connections, and end up finding it to be an exhausting process because a journey filled with caution and doubt hinders our chances to experience fulfilling and freeing moments.

Healing after disappointment is learning not to let the little things cause big roadblocks. Healing is letting nothing stop your growth; it is knowing the things that can disrupt and block your flow. Malice, blame, gossip, and negative judgment will make others take detours to avoid you, and they are the reason most two-way streets get redesigned as one way.

When the relationships you lean on for support don't have a fair balance, trying to overcompensate can hurt. Be proactive about acknowledging the changes, both in how you feel and in what you want. It starts with knowing what you need and understanding what works best for you. You may need someone to listen to you reflect. Talking things out can be how you unwind, but you can't do that if your partner is unwilling to hear you vent. The sense of unbalance conflicts with your choice to trust yourself.

You're trying to relax after a long day, but the lack of cooperation is twisting you in knots. You may desire more adventure, outings, and an active life. Your partner may enjoy staying in, having private time, and avoiding crowds. There will be instability until you find a way to compromise.

Our choices lead us to our relationships, and if we choose healthy ones these relationships continue to provide us a greater sense of direction throughout our journey. Now more than ever, it's time to feel that freedom to choose what's best for your life.

When you choose to free yourself from the past, you have to free everyone in it as well. You may not have any ill feelings, but to withhold love works against the choice to become whole. You are not letting go of the past because things are perfect in your present life. You are letting go because having peace, love, and truth matter that much to you.

Understand, you are not letting go of the past because it is easy for you, you are letting go because moving forward is what's best for you. The truth is, we are in this world to contribute love, support, and our gifts for the betterment of each other. We are living to advance through collaboration. Trust provides solid balance in the give-and- take of all efforts. Trust helps us feel secure when we let others get closer to our heart.

Some will say, "Everybody doesn't deserve to be close," and that is true. But the better you know and understand yourself, the easier it will be to see who is right for you and who is not. You will learn your friends not by who they are, but by who you desire to be.

When you are discontent and ready to change, you will want to grow out of where you are. You will want changes that bring simplicity and joy into your life. You will have a new acceptance for people who have been in a similar place and needed to make the same adjustments that you have. At some point, you won't be looking for shortcuts on your journey. You will be done with lying, pretending, and denying yourself a chance to be your authentic self. Your focus will be on growth, and you will be able to recognize people who have committed to their own growth. Look closely and you will see people like you who apply principles of truth, authenticity, love, and endurance to their development.

There is a solid quality about wholeness that improves our discernment when it comes to relationships. It does not mean every choice we make for friends, romance, and business partners will be perfect. But there is a reason we need to know every person who enters our life. Sometimes we find out why a person comes into our life in a matter of weeks or months. Other times, it takes years to see why the two of you crossed paths.

As relationships grow, there are two branches that sprout from its foundation: revelation and separation. Revelation is revealing or disclosing something that wasn't realized until the moment it passed your lips. Separation is a gap or divide; it is a point of parting.

Many things can tear a relationship apart. For most couples, without healing, the inability to bounce back from disappointment ruins the relationship. We need trust and a sense of wholeness to fight for love. Without this, the smallest of changes can affect the way we perceive our partner.

Another fold to revelation describes God revealing a greater will for your life. One that is greater than the vision you currently see in front of you. Your personal will is your purpose for living. Yet, finding your purpose may cause some pain. Discovering that you want to change may separate you from others you may have known for a long time.

Being open to extraordinary possibilities for your life at first won't feel normal. Remember that positive growth can take you on a path that you weren't expecting. And it may be taking you away from certain people you thought you needed in order to be strong. But it is also leading you to the people you need to be with in order to become whole. This is an uncomfortable branch of separation, and it happens many times in our lives.

It is true, we out-grow people we thought would always be in our lives. We no longer feel happy doing work that once brought us joy. We end relationships after hoping the fire and chemistry that brought you two together returns in some way.

The truth is, not everyone deserves to know you at every level. Some may even decide to leave you on your journey, but you are not here to make sure everyone understands your life. The people who deserve to be close are the ones who respect you and know that you don't do things that will stifle your growth.

When you make your growth a priority, the process will teach you who needs to be close to you in life. Anyone who is good for your heart will not divide you from what's best for your life. You cannot force any connections in relationships, no matter how well you know and understand yourself.

People will match what they can in an effort to be a good fit for you; and if it is not authentic, eventually you will see through it. More importantly, listen to what the other person isn't willing to do. No one wants to be in a position or situation that they cannot or will not honor. Therefore, it is wise to avoid trying to change someone who has disrespected your honor. It is not up to you to change your partner. It is up to your partner to change. If you expect honesty and he or she lies to escape discomfort, your desire for a trusting relationship will battle with their desire to feel secure. Your instinct is to change them. Instead, you can learn to see the person in front of you as they truly are. Is the love you cling to worth feeling like you don't have a grasp in life? You will know the love is real by what it inspires you to do, and healthy love will always encourage you to grow.

As you grow and learn to trust, get prepared to see everything around you from a new perspective and that includes the value of your time, the people you have in your circle, and the opportunities you consider for your life. Think of it all as new possibilities, and prepare to see life as it is. You cannot force an old flame to love you again. You cannot think about the money you could have spent in a better way. Trust requires us to let go of past expectations because it knows we need acceptance. Trust understands that not everything we love is ours to keep forever. Knowing this isn't a reason to hold back in relationships, it is instruction to value every day you get with the people who matter to you. Trust teaches us that life doesn't need our control to work out for our good. Life only asks that we stay balanced, and keep growing.

3. You Can Trust Someone

There's a common belief that "You can't trust anyone." I've heard this statement many times throughout my life. I caught my girlfriend cheating in high school; my friends told me "You shouldn't have trusted her." I lost some money in a business deal; my family told me "You shouldn't have trusted that guy."

I have heard so many different things about trust, both the pros and cons. The truth is, there are trustworthy people who we encounter every day in our lives. This doesn't mean we have to tell each individual our secrets and give them the password to our phones. But it does mean we can live with an open approach to life, and not treat those we meet as if "they are like all the rest." We can learn to trust in a way that affirms love and truth. We can be productive and patient as it develops, calling out the fake stuff for what it is and dealing with it. That means being vulnerable and uncomfortable through the process, and having fortitude even when growth seems to be a constant struggle.

Trusting relationships last when people are willing to make adjustments. Believing that you can't trust anyone will make it hard to heal from the past. You can start making progress if you adjust your attitude toward trust and remember two things. First, before anything else, believe that you can trust yourself. Second, know that you can learn who to trust in your life. You're not a fool for love. You won't need to trust everyone, but be willing to build it when it is necessary.

I speak to people daily who feel like they have no one to lean on in their difficult times. Some express feeling burnt out, others overworked, but most feel under constant pressure. Very few feel supported. It can be deflating to feel like you don't have anyone on your team. Disheartening, to feel like you're battling alone. These times happen most when you withdraw from your relationships instead of opening up. You build an imaginary wall and lament at the fact that there is no trust. But without trust, it is hard to have confidence in any support that might come your way.

We can choose to improve our relationship with trust over time; it doesn't have to be an overnight thing. It matters if you're in a rough part of life and feel defeated. It matters that you don't want to give your trust only to have it taken for granted. But what's important is growing from this season of fear and doubt. I understand if you feel like you're lacking direction and looking for a sign, asking God for help. I understand if you want another way out of the difficult times you are in. But you can redefine your moments of defeat as opportunities to define your character; you can use trust to build your determination. You can use trust to build a village of people who uplift each other. These are people who know what it is like to overcome difficulty. Trust is another way to find support, encouragement, and connection in relationships. Trusting yourself makes sure fear has no influence on who you decide to become in life. Trusting other people means fear isn't deciding who gets to stay in your life.

It helps to have a good sense of how you want your relationships to go. Emotional connections will require you to volunteer more of yourself. You may have to share your fears, uncomfortable flaws, and extend beyond your comfort zone. But it is all worth it because it creates relationships that give you confidence. The past is the past, and it should stay there. You can build the right relationships for you; you can trust someone.

4. When You Know You Know

N ew relationships will develop in your life. Trust doesn't need to be an exhausting exercise when they do. You don't have to force yourself to give, but you can trust yourself to share your heart. You can stop trying to control everything. The great relationships are going to mature day to day; there's no rushing the process. You'll know them by the way they feel; you'll sense the difference and know that it is authentic. It will be clear to you that your partner will help you grow.

Researchers published some interesting findings in the August 2014 issue of the Journal of Neuroscience. The data showed that our brains decide trustworthiness quicker than an eye blink. The study states that the exact number is three-hundredths of a second. This means that when you know, you know. You don't have to second-guess everything you feel, and you do not have to limit yourself to what's familiar. Use what you've learned to be someone better than before. Not everybody will care to teach you with love, but every person you meet knows something you can use. Embrace each person's purpose and trust the new growth in your life.

Building trust begins with understanding the layers: symmetry, awareness, and knowledge.

Symmetry addresses the balance in relationships. It helps determine the flow of power. It measures when the relationship loses a level of trust and when one is gained or restored.

Awareness is about our insight on the issues within the relationship. It is bigger than who is to blame and who is right or wrong. Being aware helps us process the intent and motivation of others when they act. Taking time to gather information, ask questions, and build some familiarity is helpful. Being aware also means looking at yourself and facing the truth. You can't make anything solid when you resort to lying to yourself. Trust should be a product of connection, never built with false hope.

Knowledge is the final layer to building trust. Every day people are learning more about the world and how it works. Most of the lessons come from very personal experiences. Knowledge allows us to better understand what's appropriate in certain situations. Knowledge helps us consider the value in a person's intentions. It helps us establish empathy before judgment, and it works as a guide.

Even with understanding the layers, trust will work differently in every relationship. Though some connections will weaken through the years, many of them can stay strong with mutual effort. Trust your relationships to be true. Build them one layer at a time.

Validation is an important part of our communication. With it, we create a space to build trust and intimacy for relationships. Validating styles of interacting can include mindful listening, open acknowledgment, and asking questions.

Mindful listening is the act of being present in each moment with kindness and without judgment. It is when you can let go of your physical and emotional reactions to what people say to you. When you are not mindful, your thoughts and worries will distract you from the moment. You may fail to see or hear what people are doing and saying. Not being attentive can make us come off as dismissive and unbothered. Both attitudes are a waste of time if you care about the person trying to get through to you. Our tendency to shut down makes 'acknowledgment and acceptance' productive tools in trust. They teach us that validating what a person says does not equal agreeing with their message.

Because we tend to see the world through the lens of our own experiences and personality, keeping strong relationships means we need to take time for empathy. We need to be able to acknowledge and understand a situation from someone else's point of view. Acknowledgment will help strengthen your relationships.

A good way to show you comprehend and that you've actually been listening is by asking questions. When we care to get closer to a person, we use questions as tools to clarify, affirm, and build trust. Questions foster good creative thinking skills and can help us make better decisions. A thoughtful question can show someone that you care about them and that you pay attention. There will be times where the people we love will express things that we don't like, understand, or agree with. We need the patience to not become defensive. Rushing to make their thoughts and feelings our own is unfair. We cannot internalize other people's moments of weakness or uncertainty, not if we want to uplift them. Asking questions can help you validate your partner if you are willing to accept their truth. Questions are for people who want to grow. Remember that trust brings us together, while lack of trust pushes us farther apart.

We tend to overthink our relationships. We don't do it to ruin things with our partners nor do we do it to create unnecessary problems. We overthink because we're scared and because we don't trust ourselves and the decisions we want to make. When we're overthinking, everybody else's opinions become more important than our own, and we are always wondering if we measure up to outside expectations.

Even now you could be thinking about not being good enough. But it is time to accept that you are more than sufficient. You don't have to overthink your value. Trust where your heart is leading you. Trust your ability to rebuild all your broken parts. Things may be coming together differently than what you thought it would be. But the best things in life will usually happen beyond your comfort zone. There are parts of you that will be easy to love. And there are parts of you that will take time to know and understand. Still, it all makes you who you are. Let yourself evolve without feeling sorry for being where you are on your journey. Trust yourself. Stop overthinking things. When you know, you know.

T**R**UCE
Part Two:
RESOLVE

5. Battle of The Sexes

T here is a divide between the men and women living today. It is not always obvious in shopping malls or at large concert festivals, but it is there. As we age and learn how things work in the world around us, the division becomes clearer. It is happening in our classrooms, boardrooms, elections, and pay scales. This division is also known as the "battle of the sexes." A fight where men and women both trade jabs of judgment, blame, pain, and fault for the dysfunction in the world and within themselves. This stance encourages a cold war that leaves no winners and has a history of turning survivors sour - but there is hope because things don't have to stay this way.

We can resolve our issues as men and women without placing blame on one another. We can work toward redeveloping a new environment for peace and connection. We can embrace our purpose as perfect counterparts for the journey of life. The route will include success, disagreement, impatience, compromise, struggle, and many other things. But it is all for the greater purpose of evolution. Every difficult situation we endure and overcome is there to be a bridge to something newer and better in life. We are all here seeking some sort of growth throughout our personal journey. It is important for us to develop a mindset that supports a communion of the sexes. We must decide that coming together is better than accepting division.

The battle of the sexes keeps us in a place where love is devalued. The primary reason is that many people are stuck in pain. When the value of love is low, traumatic experiences start to feel like routine side effects of life. When the value of love is not a priority, people don't believe they have a responsibility to grow. Less love means less appreciation for life. This is problematic because several of the solutions in our society need principles of love.

War, poverty, greed, and hate can all end using loving principles; but unfortunately, the repeated feeling of pain turns people that don't know how to heal away from love. It is hard to value love when you believe it is the reason for all your deepest agony. Holding feelings of heartache, rejection, betrayal, and abandonment perpetuates the hurt we feel in our heart.

Sometimes it seems that love in our generation is not looked at as a way of life: it is only limited to romance or what somebody does for you. Yet, love as a way of life allows us to be open, optimistic, and truthful. In spirit, we are equal and being a man or a woman is irrelevant. Both sexes contribute toward the balance for life on Earth. We can resolve our differences for the greater good of our future together. We can increase the value of love by releasing the pain in our hearts and by accepting the things that have happened in our lives as necessary events that help us grow beyond our wildest dreams.

6. An Original Plan

A ll living people are one in the same. Men and women are different by function, but created in the same love. In the creation of man, God offered both masculine and feminine energy. They were created to work together. God is the universal loving Spirit. This Spirit is the beginning of all life and the creator of the living soul. Science breaks down how a living soul develops a male or female body through conception and reproduction. And without a doubt, the creator meant for both sexes to have a mighty purpose in life. Now many ask which is better, male or female and while there are millions of theories out there on both, what matters most is what we do with our Spirit.

Everyone has a masculine and feminine balance, which refers to our nature and expression of energy. There are things that make masculine energy powerful, assertive and brilliant. There are also qualities that make it vulnerable, flawed, and scary.

God, the universal loving Spirit, offers a solution of balance in feminine energy. Masculine energy without feminine energy is not whole; it does not feel valued. Alone, it is not nurtured or appreciated, and it feels incomplete. In like manner, feminine energy without masculine energy is also not whole. It feels unsupported; it is not focused, it is scattered, busy, and unstable; it is without purpose. The function for both masculine and feminine energy is to balance the living soul. Men and women are here to grow together. We all have a personal balance to master, and we do so through appreciating the value of both sides.

We develop the strength of the masculine side by having a profound belief in the value of our own life. We promote the goodness of the feminine side by developing our belief in the value of the life of others.

If you have too much strength and not enough goodness, you can do a lot of harm to people. Yet, if you have too much goodness and very little strength, you can injure yourself, partly because you tend to give your goodness away. Both the masculine and feminine sides depend on what our inner-self has learned while becoming who we are. If you have been taught to be a bully, pushing people to the side without courtesy or respect, then your masculine side is working overtime. It wants to suppress emotions of insecurity, fear, and loneliness. The suppression alerts your feminine side to help, but it can't because you've learned to ignore it.

On the other hand, if you've learned to become a people pleaser, someone scared to make decisions for themselves in fear of disappointing anyone, your feminine side is in overdrive. You will start to feel like your best is being taken for granted. You will feel unappreciated and overlooked; you will also question the benefit of being nice. These feelings alert your masculine energy to help, but it cannot help if you ignore your strength to change.

Counterparts, Intimacy, and Acceptance

Our energy as men and women is complementary by design. It does not mean there will be absolute peace all the time, but it does mean that we can resolve several of our problems by adjusting our understanding of what caused them in the first place.

We experience too soon and develop too late.

People find pain before they get to know their purpose, they feel the sting of disappointment before they know success. Many don't condition themselves to accept the truth in fear of the pain that will likely follow. And the fear blinds them from the real cause of their pain.

When the truth says, "Robert, you don't do well with being on time." It may hurt to hear, but the truth also says, "Ask Sarah how she learned to be so punctual, she may have some tools that will work for you."

Knowing what makes you late is learning the truth. Having the awareness to be on time is using the truth. To be productive counterparts we have to use the correct tools to understand each other. Understanding is not forced or fake; it is natural and accepting.

Before fear, deceit, and evil we only knew love, harmony, and understanding. Unity with men and women starts with understanding, and it is sustained by respecting the original plan for balance and by respecting life's original design.

Some cultures view women as the assistant created for man's comfort, pleasure, and use. This idea negates our equality in the balance of life. We are not identical, but we live to complement (and sometimes compliment!) the other as perfect counterparts. In woman, God saw a complete, equal, and perfect counterpart for man.

The connection between male and female is a top priority among human relationships. Every family in the world began with a male and female connection. This union between man and woman is foundational to continuing life. It does not work divided. Men and women can know intimacy in the fullest sense of the word, far beyond sex. Sexual intimacy is not the peak of connection, but it can be the seal of a much greater intimacy; one that is more challenging to achieve. It is an intimacy that connects through the heart, soul, and Spirit to create the kind of relationship between men and women that reflects balance. This kind of relationship does not put any one person's needs as more important than the other. Relationships are about shared satisfaction and intimacy, the healthy ones give you balance, and the sick ones cause you trouble.

People confuse acceptance with approval. Somewhere in life, we learned to think that they are synonymous. They are not. For example, you could be someone who can't understand why the people you have dated are the way they are at times. Some lied, others cheated, and a few even stole from you. While you can understand them doing what they felt was necessary, and you can even accept receiving the misfortune from their decisions, none of this means you still have to keep them close.

Acceptance doesn't mean you approve of everything everyone does; it means you are done trying to change the past. It means you receive their actions for what they are. Acceptance is not only what we extend to others, but it is something we must offer ourselves. You may not be proud of every action you take, every word you speak, or every partner you choose, but in order to grow, you must accept the part of you that made a choice at that time. It will not be easy to find acceptance, feel resolve, and begin to heal, especially if you wish you could go back and make things different. But when you decide to be present, when you choose to stop hoping that you can change the past, only then will you see that acceptance prepares you to deal with the future in a balanced manner. Acceptance is the part of you that says, "I don't need a perfect hand for the cards to play in my favor."

7. Healthy Relationships Are All About Trades

In an ever-changing world, the pressure to adapt has never been greater. The pace of business is speeding up with advances in technology. Everything is digital, instant, and always changing. The flow of relationships is being disrupted by a selfish "I can replace you" mindset. For many, this threatens their idea of a good life or promising future. But, where there is threat, there is also opportunity. When a nation or group of people are trying to grow, they interchange resources as a tool. Trade is for two purposes: exchange and enrichment. Trade spurs growth between parties, it encourages specialization in particular areas of strength. The time is long overdue for men and women to come to the trading table to talk about the ways we can enrich each other through love, rather than focus on what each side is doing wrong. The question can be, "What can we all do better?" Much like a nation or company using trade for economic growth, men and women can participate too. We can use trade to improve spiritual awareness, emotional intelligence, and physical health. We can exchange ideas, affection, and recipes. We can exchange exercises, meditation techniques, and skills to maintain patience. We can choose to work together until life feels rich for each of us. As the world changes, trade and collaboration will help us to stay balanced.

Trades can go bad. It is important to know how to handle the times when they do. We have to be careful with whom we compromise; not everyone will appreciate what you are attempting to give. Learn how to change a person's role in your life without changing who you are for the worst. Even when you give the best in you, sometimes you will get excuses back. The relationship will feel unfair until you decide to balance it out. You may sacrifice time, invest money, and then have to watch your partner quit and leave. You didn't waste a trade; you learned what you should give and who deserves it. Not all trades are good trades, but honest giving always promises to attract good things back into our lives.

Trading is never perfect. People have flaws, and we all want different things out of life. Adapting quality communication skills can help you get what you want for yourself and from your relationships. Connecting is a process. A message is sent than received, processed, analyzed, and felt. Then another message is returned. This happens in the words we use, body language, and our tone of conversation. We should also be cognizant of our non-verbal communications like hand movements and facial expressions. These are things that could trigger an emotional shutdown. This does not mean we can't be ourselves and it is not an excuse to hold back. This is a reminder to be aware.

Honesty is our greatest tool in communicating. Honesty creates an efficient space to resolve a misunderstanding. At times a person's honesty can catch us off guard in a painful way. Sometimes the truth may hurt, but that's not all it does. The truth can heal, mature, lead, and teach us, and when respected, it makes room for peace, acceptance, and love. If we only allow the truth to hurt, we limit its power and purpose. When we seek the truth in each day, we grow through its guidance, and we can trade our old ways of thinking for new processes that better suit us. And even if it takes a painful comment for us to face the truth within, dealing with the feeling contributes to us gaining a renewed spirit and a clear mind. Truthful communicators are vital for any relationship that expects growth.

When our relationships aren't in a healthy place, we can move them towards a better one with behavior trades. We don't have to give up at the first sign of difficulty. With love, we can trade physical and mental abuse for encouraging and thoughtful validation. We can trade manipulation, judgment, and blame for transparency, solutions, and atonement. When a relationship is healthy, there is room for growth, and it then becomes a safe space for communication, trust, friendship, understanding, trade, and shared fulfillment.

8. Be A Mirror of Positivity

M any say pain often births purpose. Out of disappointment, failed attempts, and missed marks we learn to guide ourselves. While pain can be an effective teacher, it is not the only way we find our place in life. We learn many things from hurtful experiences but holding on to them makes it hard to see a way to move forward. Holding on to pain makes it hard to see the entirety of our self and what relationships matter. Struggle is an unavoidable part of the life experience, but we aren't meant to suffer and struggle our entire lives. We can overcome suffering by developing our endurance, and by not settling for anything less than the things we know we deserve.

We don't get to choose what we learn; we only get to choose whether we learn in joy or pain. When you look at yourself what have you learned to see? If you were to stand in front of a mirror, what do you imagine seeing reflected back? Are you thinking of your appearance? Do you hear someone else's thoughts of you or do you nick pick at yourself? The thoughts that you believe about yourself will be what you project onto others. Thinking positive affirming thoughts about yourself makes room for positive and uplifting connections to come to you.

We should remember that each experience is there to teach us something. You may not be proud of the way you had to learn the things that you know. You may be recovering from learning some things you didn't want to know. This is all in your reflection. In the mirror, you see yourself clearer than anyone else can. You know your mistakes, choices, and intentions. Don't look away from your reflection before loving what's in front of you. It may not be easy, but this decision is the foundation to your healing.

Sometimes our heart is so used to being wrong in relationships, that when we look at ourselves, we can only see the bad things. Even when the mind wants to forgive and move forward the heart doesn't let go as easy. Our heart's reasoning, as well as its feelings, depends on its moral condition. A heart full of lies, deception, and jealousy won't reflect love into relationships because it is not in a condition to give what it doesn't have. And it is important to protect our heart from this kind of negativity because it is the deepest part of our being– it is the whole of who we are. Much as our eyes are to see and our ears to hear, the heart is used to understand, to discern, and to give us insight.

There are some things that get in the way of being a mirror of positivity. We are in an era where anything can get shamed. Religion, education level, sexual preference, and the idea of a perfect career path are just a few. It can all be an excuse for shame. We use things like social media to be an extension of our voice in the world. Sometimes it is done with sensitivity, and more often we say what we want without thinking. Shame is a word that carries a lot of weight, but it shouldn't be something you burden yourself with. Shame is the painful feeling that arises when you're aware you've done something wrong, like when you know you've done something improper or ridiculous. Shame is not meant to be a form of oppression; it is only felt through personal choice. Nobody can make you feel guilty about something you know is good. And nobody can hide you from shame when it comes to something you know is bad. If shame is what you feel when you look in the mirror, it is time to figure out why, so you can grow.

Shame and self-doubt are tools used as destroyers in relationships. These things interfere with our ability to be mirrors of positivity for our partners and ourselves. When you only reflect on the wrong done to you in the past, it makes it hard to focus on good things in the present. Look up and realize where you are, who you are, and the relationships that matter to you. Is the shame you feel worth the cloud over your head? Is being afraid of a new beginning worth keeping the same old complaints? Many relationships fail because of unresolved insecurity issues and people being unwilling to speak up. When we avoid new opportunities to change, the past will repeat itself. Holding confusion and guilt in our heart will ruin the relationships that matter to us the most.

If there are people who think a relationship will go wrong, then there are also those frightened of a connection going right. Some people believe anything that goes right is too good to be true. When the horizon shows a new morning all they can think of is how it won't last. So they sabotage love, and many do so with their words. They say things like, "this will never work" or "it is only a matter of time before things goes bad." The anxiety attached to failure is about rejection and the heavy feeling that comes after creating a bond with someone only for it to be one-sided. It is the emptiness felt after giving your all and getting seemingly nothing in return. We start to punish ourselves after disappointment through our relationships. We don't want to get attached to the wrong person, so we stop believing we know how to choose the right one. However, when we let the dread of failure go, we learn to focus on the elements of success. Trust me; you have everything in you to make the relationships that you need work. Don't let the pain of your past distort your view of reality in the present.

43

Don't start pushing people away that bring you joy. Harmony, longevity, and love need trust, not control, not fear. If you don't believe in you with all your heart, somebody in tune with your reflection will feel that. And when they do, stop being scared and let them be the support you need.

Everything that surrounds you is in relationship to you in some shape or form. Your living soul connects to the Spirit of all life. How you perceive things is very fundamental and affects your experience in relationships. Changing perception and developing resolve begins with a mind shift. Mind shifts deal with the whole truth without stopping at the parts that make us uncomfortable. We spend too much time trying to compartmentalize things for comfort. Healing after disappointment is learning to let go of the comfort zone. Love is being willing to see old things in a new way, through conversation, presence, even taking a minute to appreciate a smell. We have to value life, in all its forms and beauty. Everybody is claiming to have a solution for happily ever after that sounds more appealing than the other. Mine is simply – be a mirror of positivity in your relationships. As you mature and your perception of the world changes, remember to shine your light. Know that you can be both flawed and cherished.

9. Truth Is The New Romance

If you're reading this book, you've figured out at some point in life that you aren't living in a fairytale. Some parts of your life have hit you hard, and out of nowhere. Hollywood and "popular culture" have changed what people think relationships should look like. Some believe social media creates unhealthy dynamics for relationships. But social media does not ruin strong relationships it only exposes the weak ones. The trends of the world, what we share on our social media accounts, it is all a reflection of shared consciousness. Movies, television shows, entertainment all represent an imitation of life. Often these outlets create a perception versus reality divide that can be hard to maneuver in love. Hollywood sells the dream. Their ploy for emotional connection is romance. And though it feels good, getting lost in passion can be a dangerous cycle. Many who do often call themselves, "hopeless romantics." We look at the screen and say, "Why can't you be more like that?" Or "Why can't my life be more like his or hers." This creates a negative culture of comparison and gives power to the idea that we all have to be the same or in trend to be valuable. We don't need fairy tales to have the real thing, for only God narrates Bona fide love.

45

The topic of closure comes up often in my conversations with people experiencing difficult breakups. Closure is not romantic. Often the person is searching for a reason about why things did not go the way they desired. They feel displaced and want an end or conclusion to the situation. They pose the idea of needing closure, and in it, they are searching for a point of resolve. Closure hopes that the past has a perspective that will make it easier to move forward. But you can't stay with something that no longer exists. The past is what it was; your life is in today. Closure is a personal decision, not a mutual agreement. There is always another "why" and more "ifs." The truth is that you had a loving relationship for some time. It ended, whether it was money, distance, or planning- it is over now. The best option for closure is to accept the truth without wishing you could change it.

Acceptance alleviates us of the pressure to change other people. Regardless of how much we care about a person, we cannot force a relationship with them. Everyone won't always be who you want and need them to be. It is not romantic to face this, but it is the truth. There are things we can do to boost acceptance in our relationships, gestures that help in moving forward. In these cases, the greatest gesture of closure is an apology. It is a moment to restore faith with honesty, and a new foundation for trust. When you choose to accept and forgive a person, go all the way, or it will not work. Rebuilding trust is not something that works half committed or one-sided.

When we stop searching for closure, we can look to see how we are being redirected in life. The end of one thing is the beginning of another. Growth is learning to embrace the new beginnings with enthusiasm. It is having knowledge of who you are and staying committed to loving. The most romantic thing any of us can do is have peace with who we are.

Truth is the new romance because truth lasts. The truth doesn't need dressing up; it isn't for show, or occasional. The truth is consistent. Consistency is romantic. When you can look your partner in their eyes and see an affirming reflection, one that says, "I hear you, and I get it." That's intimacy and the essence of romance. The truth is romantic because it always gives opportunity for accountability and amends. The truth is always ready to work with you to make good things better. If the truth ever breaks something valuable to you, be thankful because it is now time for something more, something greater.

10. Getting Your Worth

There is a business motto that says, "You don't get what you're worth, you get what you negotiate." In love, unlike business, you do get your worth. The negotiation happens in your heart. Part of your heart yearns for comfort and something familiar. Another part is searching for adventure and fulfillment. Some days you may feel divided and uncertain about what is best for you. But one particular day you'll stop second-guessing. It may be after a series of disappointing relationships; it may be the loss of a loved one or the blessing of a new child. You'll know the feeling, and you will recognize the time. This is your soul choosing a spirit of resolve and resiliency. Your worth begins and ends with what you give yourself. You have to be able to last long enough to get what you believe is yours.

Getting your worth means you need to care with passion. It is a process that requires you to be all in, both feet, undivided. Love will help you build up the resolve necessary to get what's yours. When you want something with an intense desire, only you can stop yourself from having it. Be passionate in your relationships and about your growth. Knowing your worth is pointless if you're always willing to compromise your value.

Getting your worth means ignoring the odds. Sometimes it takes blind optimism to outlast the obstacles that confront us in life. When you submit to odds, opinions, and outside limitations you're not trusting yourself. It doesn't matter what happened before. Your soul doesn't need the unnecessary pressure of the past. The odds don't matter. There has never been this version of you before now. Be happy – that odds are irrelevant.

Prepare to endure some challenging situations. If plan A doesn't work, use plan B as a way to help it. And plan C to find another, D for another, and so forth until it works for you. Resolve, like belief is a powerful force that lives within us all. We have the power to transform negative situations into awesome opportunities. No pain can last forever and it is true, "What doesn't kill you will only make you stronger." The first plan may not be the best one. But with resolve, you won't stop until you have one that works for you. Be comfortable and reassured from the fact that your resolve can increase when you want it to. The challenges are only preparing you to manage the blessings ahead. Trust who you are becoming.

T R U C E
Part Three:
UNDERSTANDING

11. You Never Know How Your Lesson Will Show Up

Living a healthy life isn't about trying to avoid difficult times. Being strong comes from understanding struggle. The experiences that teach us are God's investment in our future. Whether the circumstance today feels right or wrong, we're still here to grow. Sometimes the growth is going to hurt and feel uncomfortable and walking our path may look different than we thought it would. But growing in life means understanding when to make adjustments. Every day is an opportunity to mature and learn.

"Hope for the best but prepare for the worst," is a motto people use in times of uncertainty. Hoping for the best is something I do with natural zeal because I enjoy feeling capable - like things are going to work out. Preparing for the worst is something I've taught myself to do before feeling helpless. No matter how we prefer things to feel day to day, life conditions us to be ready for whatever. It is not what happens to us that makes the biggest difference; it is how we respond to it. If we are willing to change and to flourish, we can never be helpless, so it doesn't matter if it is the best or worst times. Unfortunate things are going to happen, but misfortune does not make us incapable. We can use it to refine our aim. We can expect to learn something useful every day of our lives. We can prepare to be moldable, balanced, and open-minded. When we increase our understanding of the world, and we don't need mottos to manage our feelings. We embrace the moment and whatever emotions it may bring. Then we release them so that we can focus on what we want most: Growth. We can use challenging times as a chance to increase our focus.

Staying focused is easier to do when things are going well. After disappointment, it is hard to focus on anything outside of how it feels to be let down. Getting our hopes up can be exhausting. Trusting, resolving personal issues and preparing to open up again takes strength. As we rebuild and grow our excitement for healing, we have to be ready for different tests. Life will feel like it is testing everything about us. Life tries our knowledge, faith, and understanding. Keep going. Don't spend time with fear; it is the biggest energy drainer. Being scared and feeling damaged can make starting over again seem too risky. With fear the focus shifts from growing in life to avoiding another chance of getting hurt. Trying to control which lessons happen and which don't block growth and maturity. Fear is an enemy to focus. Fear doesn't want us balanced and stable with our emotions. Fear wants to keep us distracted and depressed. It doesn't want us to understand what we're dealing with on the inside. But we deserve to be at peace with ourselves. We all deserve more than turmoil, uncertainty, and mistrust. It may not be easy staying focused with so many things going on in life, but it can be done.

In times of misunderstanding, it can be a test talking to people we care about. Life has a way of making us feel twisted in knots. And when we are wound up and stressed after disappointment it is hard to see who's who. It is hard to tell who understands and who's faking that they do. When we're scared or feel damaged, we don't want the risk of being vulnerable. We don't want to be transparent and have it used against us later. The thought of being misunderstood can keep us from being authentic. The fear of things going wrong can stop us from acknowledging our real feelings. But suppressing real emotions isn't healthy for anyone. You feel everything you're feeling right now for a reason. Confused, wound up, stressed out, whatever the case. Use this as a moment of motivation to let it out and talk about it. Attempt to articulate what is happening within. It is okay if you don't like to talk about things right after they happen. But it is important to understand how talking about things can help in healing. Even if it means writing your thoughts out before conversation.

53

Holding negativity in only means it is still with us to hurt us again later. Our pain builds walls as protection, and those same walls end up either falling on us or dividing us from our healing. When we release negativity, we break down a barrier in the way of our growth. When we learn to forgive, we dismantle anything trying to impede our peace. Breaking down these walls is critical to understanding who we are. It is vital to healing after disappointment. Healing is always about moving forward and growing. It is about spiritual, physical, and emotional balance. Everything around us affects our balance. The food we eat, the time of the day and the weather in different seasons. We are always influenced by our environment and the people in it, and we never know what these people are there to teach us about life. We do know that we're here right now living for a reason, and it isn't to be hurting. Regardless of how the lessons show up, we can't miss them because we're numb and blinded by our pain. We can't be so tuned into the negativity that we let unnecessary walls block the blessings coming our way. If we are going to save anything for later, it should be room to see the beauty in change.

12. How To Hear Again

M ost communication is nonverbal. What we say and how we say it matters, but the majority of what we express happens without words. It is a combination of body language, posture, and different gestures. With so many ways to communicate, knowing how to receive messages is important. Slouched shoulders, tension around the eyes, lip biting, it all says something. We read into these behaviors in hopes of better understanding the person in front of us. What is it that they want, what are they trying to say, and do they mean any of it? Knowing how to receive what people say to you can be the difference in keeping them close or not.

People tend to assume they are better at listening than they are. In reality, most people only listen to what they want to hear. We learn how to tune in and out of conversations to protect ourselves. It is called selective hearing. We half listen, skimming through to pick up what we need to know for a basic understanding. But the goal of listening is to have a full understanding of what a person is saying. Selective hearing doesn't give us the thorough comprehension needed to make real changes. It only shows us how to see symptoms; it doesn't teach us their cause. Healing is about making real changes. It is fixing the things that cause us to lose balance, tune others out, and get defensive. To be a good friend, lover, and a good parent - we need to listen so that we can understand because understanding is what improves relationships. Through listening, we develop a connection to what's going on around us. And during the process of healing, listening is how we learn to get stronger.

One of the greatest gifts we can offer someone is our ears with an open heart. Listening without judgment is a way we affirm our partner's value as a person. It is a moment of acceptance, understanding, and love. We are holding up a mirror so they can see and hear unfamiliar parts of themselves. We listen to understand, and we use understanding to become better people. We listen to find the truth, and we use the truth when we want to build lasting relationships. We listen to learn, and we use everything we gain to grow. Listening is a chance to discover things we don't know. It is also an opportunity to learn something that will expand our perspective. When we take the time to hear people out it sends a message that says it is okay to be yourself.

When we encourage people to be themselves, it is unfair to box them in with assumptions. We can't assume we know what's on their mind or in their heart.

We can't expect things will go the same way they always have with them. People change everyday. Especially after they're hurt. We need the patience to learn and understand why certain changes are necessary. We need the focus and empathy to listen with an open heart. When our thinking is not blocked by premature assumptions, we make stronger connections. When we're free to be our full self, we recognize how uplifting mutual understanding can feel.

We listen differently when we care about the person speaking. And when we have a personal investment in what is being expressed. When a message is to our benefit, we make sure to acknowledge it in its entirety. We make sure to be attentive. Yet, when we're feeling attacked, threatened, or uncomfortable it is hard to stay open. We can't hear what we need to because on the inside we're too busy trying to figure a way out of feeling shame, guilt, or embarrassment. Our attention shifts from being open to receive what's being spoken to using our ego as a shield, blocking mutual understanding.

When our emotions are off balance, we tend to rely on listening filters for comfort. The filters each have a different function, but they all count in communication. For example, there are times where we're listening to a person, and the only thing we can think of is what we're going to say next. We use a filter that teaches us to listen with the intent to respond, not with the attention to receive. Other times we're only looking to defend or prove we're right and what the other person is saying is wrong. This filter shows up when we would rather show we're strong than stay connected. Some conversations are direct and concise; others take a longer time to get cleared up. When we're low on patience in these situations we use a filter that says, "Get to the point." It rushes the person to share information that may not have been fully processed or vetted. And while this filter may save time, it doesn't improve the stability of the relationship.

The filters we use depends on the internal conversation going on in our mind at the time. If we're beating ourselves up, comparing, and nitpicking then the voice we'll hear other people through is one of criticism and put-downs. They could say something simple like, "I don't like the gift you bought me." And what we would receive is, "If I made more money and were a better partner, I would've gotten the right gift." When we're not secure, no matter the guidance, wisdom, or opinion, it all feels like harsh criticism. Our self-doubt activates, and it has an adverse influence on the way we filter the things we hear. Simple conversations aren't so simple anymore after the fear of not being enough enters our thoughts. Instead of being open, we shut down and worry. After every discussion, we spend time wondering if our companion still loves us or if they want to leave. And it is unhealthy always trying to please someone who has shown that they don't care how you are feeling inside. When we listen to "Make everything okay" we may risk denying the truth to keep someone we don't need in our lives anymore.

There is another type of listening that can help us as we navigate throughout life. It is listening to the spirit, our internal teacher. Though our feelings and fears may change with each day, the Spirit of life is consistent. Anytime we hear our spirit speaking it is significant. It is there to help us enjoy life and become the best version of who we can be. It speaks to guide us throughout life and to show us who people are. Our spirit talks about the lessons we need to watch out for. It speaks of the work that will fulfill us. After disappointment, when nobody else can give us what we need to hear, our spirit speaks up and says, "I believe in you, you got this, keep going."

As I grew older and learned to persevere in life, prayer became more important to me. I often heard the phrase, "Pray about it" when stressed or confused. But more often than not I only used prayer as a way to vent and express my frustrations with life. As I worked to change myself, the way I understood prayer changed as well. Now I understand prayer is much more like meditation than anything else. Praying gives us a chance to hear God's guidance and instruction. It is hard to do that talking the entire time. Prayer isn't about what we have to say; it is an act of listening. And there is no perfect way to pray, but I've learned to speak no more than five to ten minutes and to listen for no less than thirty. Each day, we can become more mindful, aware, and healthy. By listening, we can learn how to hear love again.

13. A Spirit Is Strengthened When It Serves Another Spirit

S hortly before he passed away, my grandfather told me a story. He said that there are two lions living inside of us. They both fight for power in our lives. One represents our higher nature; it stands for kindness, courage, and love. The other represents the lower nature of things like greed, hate, and fear. When I asked my grandfather which lion was strongest, he replied, "The one we feed."

Whatever we feed grows and whatever we starve dies. When we feed into negativity and spiteful actions, drama and confusion inevitably grow out of it. When we feed into positivity and self-respect, love and opportunity spread from it. The things we focus on only become stronger. We can do the work of rebuilding our strength, reclaiming our worth, and being present. But only if we stop concentrating on things like rewriting the past and trying to change people. After disappointment, it is important to zone in on feeding our desire for healing. The goodness in our spirit is always working to guide, support, and keep us secure as we find our way. This part of us craves justice and looks beyond itself for meaning. Goodness is the part of us that wants to improve the world, build communities, and create beautiful works of art. It writes, paints, and supports truth. When we feed our goodness, it expands in our lives. But when we're hurting, we all are susceptible to feeding into our lower nature. And when we do there's a tendency to overemphasize our weakness and downplay the reality of our strength. We're human, and everybody has his or her time with doubt. As people who want to develop, we should embrace these moments to show our advancement. We can't change the past; we only can be better moving forward. Accept it for what it is. Feeding into envy, comparison, and feelings of unworthiness won't help in the healing process. We are not broken people. We are not powerless, depressed, or less than. Gaining strength and continuing to grow comes from feeding the goodness inside of us.

There are times where life has us saying, "I don't understand myself at all." In these moments when our confusion has reached a crescendo, it can create internal conflict with our positive self-image. Relationships can be traumatic. One day we're in love and planning our life with someone. Then another day it is over, and that's it. Losing something that seemed built to last isn't easy. Trying to do well but having things go sideways can be tough to accept. Without understanding, we can start to question and over analyze things within ourselves. And we can penalize people over problems they didn't create. Confusion is real. We all feel down or lost at times, so it is nothing to look at with shame. It is okay if we feel more than we can put into words. Uncertainty is nothing to confront with an attitude of superiority or judgment. It is a chance to say, "I'm still learning and growing, with time I'll understand what I need to."

There is a spiritual battle for our heart because it controls the things we do in relationships. There's the side of love and then the side of fear. One wants us to have unison with others, and the other wants us to be lonely. Every relationship represents either love or fear. Each person reflects something we love within ourselves and something we don't. The people encouraging us to become better, the ones talking about ideas and not other people- they're using their spirit to strengthen ours. When we make time to fellowship, share knowledge, and challenge others to be excellent, we are serving something greater than ourselves. When we choose to stay on the side of love, our actions strengthen and improve other spirits in the world. The ones who keep love in their heart have learned the most authentic way to be strong in spirit.

No matter how strong we are, there's going to be things capable of bringing us down, especially when we want to start opening up again. A modern Bible verse says, "The spirit is willing, but the flesh is weak." The flesh is the reminder of our lower, more primal and independent nature. After disappointment, this part of us is ego-driven, hurt, and stubborn. It is influenced by the fear in our heart, not the courage of love. Our lower nature "Doesn't care" about growing. It is always loud about two things: worry and stress. And if we're not aware enough to silence it, the noise it makes can drown out the true desires of our spirit. Healing is making sure our higher loving nature gets to work and show how effective it can be in our lives. Our higher nature always wants to grow, evolve, and thrive. It is willing to learn, remold, and rise with overwhelming strength.

As we learn to rise out of our difficult times, the appreciation we carry for those who've done the same increases. We begin to identify with people who've worked to liberate themselves from the past. We draw energy and strength from people who've overcome their fears of starting over. Whether it is direct or not, people leave impressions on us. As we grow, we need to be aware of who we allow to leave lasting ones.

We all mature at different paces through our seasons of struggle. There are going to be some instances in relationships where it isn't easy to find common ground. So when seeking understanding with someone, we have to be empathetic. Empathy is knowing how to identify emotions. It is compassion, feeling, and insight. Empathy is the comfort of mutual understanding. It is the assurance that we feel when we're around somebody who's been through similar experiences. When we're empathetic, we seek to understand above anything else. With empathy the goal is to see things from another person's view, it is not about getting them to see things our way. Empathy is proof our perspective and thinking can evolve. It helps us make healthy changes within ourselves. When we commit to being present in the moment, and when we listen with compassion, we're empathetic. When we're hurting and need help, fighting but want peace, the answer is empathy.

Our spirit is strongest when we give without expecting something in return. When we are full we don't count everything we share; we are more liberal. After disappointment, we tend to feel robbed and set up for failure- like someone stole things from us. Part of healing is realizing that nobody can take anything from us that we aren't supposed to do without. We don't have to count the things that we left in the past. It doesn't mean we are ignoring their value to us. It means we accept that not everything we love is ours to keep forever. Knowing this is not a reason for us to stop giving and growing in life. When we can't find the strength to give in a new relationship, then we must use the energy we have to refine ourselves. We can give ourselves encouragement without expecting an easy journey. We can give ourselves time to heal and restore without assuming a fairytale ending. Genuine giving is a sign that a person is strong. It is a sign that they are self-aware and secure. What are you willing to give yourself? Relationships with people are going to change. But the relationship we have with our spirit needs to remain consistent. Our spirit strengthens when it serves another spirit. Instead of becoming selfish people, we can be more mindful of who we share with. If we're going to continue healing, we can't stop giving.

14. Learning To Let Go

In healing the ultimate goal is to live a healthy life. It is to have balance between the physical, spiritual, and emotional parts of ourselves. This balance helps us to be energetic, vibrant, and faithful as we move forward in life. The dark relationships, old friendships, and disappointments of the past can stay there. They all happened for a reason, and they're no longer happening for a greater one. Healthy living means letting go of the negativity, hate, and resentment within. Letting go to welcome love, support, and awareness in life. The people who hurt us didn't do so with the power to keep us broken and in pain forever. It may have been difficult to see things that way at first, but it's time to put those memories behind you for good. We heal to feel life in a way that tells us, "Things are better than before." We heal to understand the people in our relationships with more insight than before. If they always caused you to question your stability and worth, then they were no good for your balance. Letting go is going to help you regain yourself.

At times we need solitude to restore our sense of direction. The process may require us to be still and slow down our busy schedules so that we can focus in on what's important. We need to be sure about what we want next. We need time to figure out how we want to feel about life. Solitude isn't about being antisocial. It is about taking the time to be good to ourselves. Sure, iron sharpens iron. But sometimes we need to take our space so that we can sharpen without cutting people we care about. Sometimes we need time alone to address and care for our wounds. We need time alone to recharge without anyone asking, "Why are you acting different?" It is not an act; it is that our restored spirit doesn't move the same as our hurt one did. Solitude is a process that teaches us what to do with our time, gifts, and love. When we know what to do with ourselves, we can let go of the people who mishandle us.

From this process of solitude comes an outflow of compassionate service to others. Those of us who feel capable have developed a strong desire to give because we've learned how to help ourselves in many ways. We understand the importance of empowering others and helping where we need to. Some situations are unfortunate, and we won't be able to solve every problem for every person we care about, but we can be beside them during their times of struggle. Sometimes we will have comforting words to say and others we will be there to listen. As we heal we learn to give beyond the pain and fear that once confined us and we get to think beyond the people who didn't recognize the value in us. Solitude and service are both about giving our spirit what it needs the most- love.

Healing is a process that happens in different ways. The scars we get over the years show we can endure pain. No matter if it is scratched, bruised, or wounded, our skin has an action plan for healing itself when we hurt. Our heart and spirit must develop the same manner, no matter what life throws our way. We can be uncomfortable with our scars at first. But we should look at these scars as evidence of a healed wound, a mark of growth. The treated skin is stronger than the skin that existed before the injury. This means when we heal, not only are things different forever but we are stronger than ever. When we heal, not only is our spirit lifted, but we can know ourselves better. The best way we heal from the past is when we open our heart up to the future. It is when we trust ourselves instead of doubting why things happen the way they do. Keep going ahead.

We're healed when we understand our heart well enough to open it. And when we're comfortable with who we are and the things we don't know. Not because we're immune to emotional pain but because we know how to turn it into a powerful lesson. Not everything that hurts us intends to break our heart, some of it happens to open our mind. The healed perspective looks at the experiences we go through with a scope of purpose. But when we keep a hurting perspective, we only view life through fear and assumptions. Healing is using our spiritual progression to retrain our mental processing. A renewed mind will improve our lives tremendously because it talks directly to the heart. Reminding it to let go of the baggage, frustration, and beliefs that cause us to constrict and avoid showing who we really are.

15. It Is About Mutual Respect

We heal in life through mutual respect. We don't always need to agree with why someone feels the way they do. But we should appreciate what it feels like to be going through something that isn't easy to handle. We should respect how quick the tables can turn in life. We should recognize what it feels like to face disappointment, betrayal, and setbacks. This respect isn't about approval or judgment; it is used to increase understanding. The painful events we experience make it hard to think about opening up and giving. Fear makes us self-centered. But this doesn't mean we have to become selfish people. When we love from a healed place, we are more inclined to be understanding and to put oneself in another's place. Doing this gives way to deeper connections and helpful alliances. Mutual respect is about learning how to grow together with harmony.

In loving someone, it is our duty to make them aware of the things that they don't see. And though it is hard to grow with anyone who doesn't want to change, we aren't wrong for wanting to help the people we love. But when it starts hurting us to help, then it is not authentic help, rather it is a form of self-sabotage. And sometimes we don't even see that we are doing it at the moment. We give away what we need and tell ourselves it is better off with someone else. We fall for people who don't deserve us, and we tell ourselves they won't survive if we leave them. This isn't fair to our heart. Being generous and selfless doesn't mean we deserve to be the ones who always come last. We shouldn't have to view giving as something that empties us, rather as something we grow from. And we shouldn't pretend to be content, or feel the need to fake our happiness. There's no healing in pretending. Making things right is an all in effort, and we have to change before we expect anyone else to. When we see unhealthy cycles, we have to address them. When we start feeling like we aren't enough, we have to focus on self-love. Trying to grow within a relationship doesn't work if both sides don't see room for change.

Acting as if we're "okay" when we aren't feeling well is the recipe to feeling worse. We only hurt more when we sit idle with pain. We only hurt more when we don't acknowledge the things that agitate and unsettle us. Still, sometimes our ego makes us think holding everything in is the best option. Rather than show we're affected and hurt, we try to show we're unbothered. It is dangerous because our ego is always selfish, short-sighted, and impatient. Our ego doesn't come out and say, "Hey I'm the part of you that hates yourself. I'm going to blind you and ruin everything." It poses as self-love, it shows up where we see ourselves as strong - to create a sense of pride. Instead of being truthful the ego is all about the opposite – faking. It doesn't care about staying balanced; it is all about self-gratifying moments. And though sometimes it can feel safe to rely on, the ego is our own power turned against us. The same part of it that sets us up to do wrong will then punish us because we did so. To love without ego should be the goal, and we only get close through discipline. We find healing through openness, by having the courage not to fake about our pain.

After disappointment, it is okay if we need a break in the normal routines of life to reassess things. It is healthy to make time to stop and gather ourselves. This isn't a break in the sense of laziness or an escape from real life. This is a break in the sense of rest from trying to work things out - a chance to rejuvenate. It is a break from pointless drama and from placing unnecessary pressure on relationships. During a break, we have time to retool, plan, and gain composure. In an NBA finals game, no matter how intense or close the score is, even that contest will have several breaks. They will break for water, TV commercials, and at the end of each quarter. Breaks are part of life, and we should take them when things aren't going right or else we are going to crash trying to force ourselves into places we shouldn't be. We should not get so consumed with having things our way that nothing natural can grow. There will be seasons where separation is the only remedy to heal our heart. In these periods we are given time to see our needs in a more accurate way. In this time we use a break as a pit stop, a moment to get ourselves stronger for the journey. There will be a time where closeness feels like harmony again. But that can only happen if we are willing to change. If we are willing to be different, then new possibilities open up in life.

When we're willing to adjust what gives us personal peace at times for the greater cause of love, we mature. Pride and ego are the enemy of understanding, connection, and progress. We need to be willing to adjust our ears and hearts to tune them out when they creep into our thoughts. We should encourage ourselves to always be ready to see a new perspective. Growth is going to stretch us. Healing is going to change things within our lives, but we will be stronger because of what we endured. When we face uncomfortable times, we can face them with balance and poise. We can take a break to make time for solitude because slowing down is a power move. And understanding pace is proof of maturity.

Nowadays pain tends to be the fuel of choice when people are looking for motivation to grow. I hear many people reference how the rigidness of life turned them into an improved person once they stopped expecting anything to be easy. Much of the pain we know in life comes from not healing from disappointment, it comes from not knowing how to bounce back. But sometimes the ugly reminders that we've been overlooked, doubted, and hated, spark the true fighter within us. The one that wants to work with love and mutual respect. We can gain strength through understanding, and sustain it when we act with empathy. When we're ready to grow, when we realize we're all in this together, then we can get clarity on the best way to move forward.

TRU<u>C</u>E
Part Four:
<u>C</u>LARITY

16. We Don't Need Everything All At One Time

S ometimes we are not aware of how our desires can affect those around us. What we do with pride, greed, and selfishness can hurt others. And it isn't always going to be intentional. Considering our wants and beliefs before others show that we respect who we are. But making our desires and beliefs the only things that matter shows that we are hurting. Selfishness is rarely a mature quality; it is limited. But being selective is a quality of growth and strength; it is progressive. Healing means being selective. Staying balanced means managing our desires on a daily basis. We'll often reflect within and have to ask the question, "Why do I want this now?" Let's be honest - we don't need everything all at one time. The increments in place are there for a reason.

After the end of a disappointing relationship, we can feel the need to make up for lost time. Our pride tells us anything that happened outside of what we wanted was a waste and now we're behind. But that's not real. The reality and the truth are that it is important to be patient with our desires. It is important for us to see the value in both the painful and beautiful lessons that life brings. It is important to give ourselves time for things to come together the way they are meant to be. There is no perfect timetable for healing our hearts or improving our relationships. Things get better when we are better. When we have a consistent desire to improve ourselves, then we start to see improvements in the relationships we choose throughout our lives.

There are real desires, things we want for ourselves that also have a positive effect on those around us. Like after a discouraging relationship, we can develop a passion for encouraging others. Or when we learn a new trade or skill, we can grow a desire to teach and share with loved ones. Sometimes when we want more for ourselves, the effort put into that desire attracts an abundance for those around us. Still, there will be times where we are feeling unsure about what's best. There will be times where we doubt what we want. In those moments, it can feel like there is a war happening between our heart and our mind. But that is only fear and ego trying to get us to work against ourselves. Something inside wants satisfaction right now, and another thing says, "Consider the bigger picture." When we say our heart and our minds are at war, it is a sign we are not trusting ourselves. When we let this lack of confidence heighten, it can affect relationships on all levels - romantic, platonic, professional, and more. We cannot let brief moments of weakness stop our pursuit of healing and gaining clarity. We cannot allow our disappointments to overshadow our innermost desires. Love, success, family, whatever it is you want most- keep going toward it. Our self-determination matters more than any opinion or judgment. When we choose to live authentic to who we are, it inspires others to define their own fulfillment as well.

We give the heart credit, or in some cases, the blame for many of our decisions. When things are going well we are warm and open with our heart; we love to follow it. When things are adverse and tumultuous, we shut down our hearts for safety. Learning to guard our heart is more important to healing than placing blame. When we can protect another person's heart with the same passion we use to defend our own, that's love. Following our heart is about growing beyond the pain in our lives. It is about giving ourselves some credit for still standing after all the blows.

Everything we do in some way flows from our heart. Our heart is the part of us that holds love the highest. It always sees new possibilities and options to grow, like when we hear a great story of triumph, one where somebody meets a true sense of accomplishment. We will hear a mention of trusting and following their heart when everything was on the line. When we hear our loved ones speak of disappointment, they may talk about how it felt opening their heart. Some will say it is a wise thing to do and others will say it created the hurt that followed. However, no one will be able to say that the experience didn't teach them a valuable lesson.

In life, not everything goes our way every time. We can choose to respond to fear and ego, or we can adopt an attitude of confidence and resilience. When we decide to trust our hearts and to keep an open mind, finding healing is inevitable.

There's a voice we hear deep inside, and it is there to guide us. Some call it our conscience, others say it's a gut feeling. Regardless of the name used, that voice is our inner teacher. It is the voice encouraging us to do better, to love, learn, grow, forgive, and evolve. When we are low on motivation, this voice reminds us that we can get through anything. When our spirit is hurting, this voice tells us that the damage is not permanent. Much like our physical wounds, when our spirits have damage we need time and love to heal. If not, we will become destructive to ourselves and our relationships. Though we may be in a rush for things to go our way, we must always consider the guidance from within. We cannot ignore the voice inside of us suggesting peace, empathy, and patience. It is there to show us how to heal and move forward in life. We have to want to see it.

We can learn to see disappointment in a way that doesn't cause destructive behaviors or bring us down. We can use the vision from our hearts to build constructive habits that assist us in letting go of old problems, assumptions, and negativity. When we see our love life moving forward, we can envision peace, harmony, and support. We don't have to limit ourselves to arguments, jealousy, and hate. When we meet someone instead of thinking it is going to be the same as last time, we can remind ourselves that we are no longer in the same space as last time. Before we self-sabotage, we can choose to see beyond our own fear and failures. By doing this, we change our perception of disappointment, and we can improve our lives.

Positive words bring positive results. We don't have to hold ourselves hostage with words of doubt and pessimism. In fact, these things make communicating into something people avoid. It is hard to get anywhere with a person set on lying, judging, complaining, and being negative. It is frustrating to talk to someone who doesn't care to say anything positive; someone only stuck on what's going wrong and the things that could get worse. Listening to excessive complaining is exhausting. There is so much good in life, and if we don't see enough positivity, then it is our duty to create more.

Changing our thinking, adjusting our speech, and using the right words will be real work, but these personal transformations happen in their own time. We become better people with diligence, patience, and fortitude. We don't have to let life bog us down. The clarity we need to feel positive, enthusiastic, and healthy comes after clearing the old worries out. Whatever has been persistent enough to create a state of worry for us, it is time to change it. The job that is not rewarding, the friend who is not respectful of your feelings, or that habit you have of not speaking up to "keep the peace." It is time to confront everything that could come between us embracing our higher, truer nature. We deserve to feel confident, self-aware, and wise in our decision-making. We deserve to know ourselves as strong, capable, and worthy of love. It may take time for things to feel as good as we dreamed they once would, but time aids in healing. Growth is a gradual, graceful process. We don't need everything all at one time.

17. Prepare A Place For Peace

When we have clarity of self, we don't have to fight for acceptance, approval, or value. We are who we are, and the people capable of loving us will recognize that. We all get hurt, pain is part of the physical life experience, it is no more reserved for the worse than it is for the good. We can look at painful circumstances as challenges rather than punishments. They are moments meant to make us stronger rather than moments designed to break us for having flaws. It is unhealthy viewing life from an "I'm the victim, and they're wrong" perspective. We've all done wrong, and most of us will agree that we know misfortune all too well. But dwelling here only leaves us with unhappiness and discontent. Healing is when our pain transfers into a definite purpose. It is when we see ourselves as deserving of love, trust, and fulfillment.

Avoiding pain won't teach us how to grow, the only way we get better is by facing the things that hurt. Acknowledging fear, insecurity, and personal shortcomings can revitalize our clarity. Not everyone wants to harm us. We don't have to live life in fear that it will be painful every time we fall in love. Instead of letting the discord break us, we will use the lesson as a building block, gaining confidence one step at a time.

Our motivation for love has to come from a desire to grow positively. Dealing with pain is where we gain empathy, understanding, and knowledge. It is how we master the path to get better, and it is how we help each other mature and improve.

Good love exists beyond our fallen hopes. Though the possibility isn't popular to believe in after disappointment, real love and authentic relationships are still around and obtainable. We can stay true to our deepest desires for love, trust, and commitment. We can refuse the choice to lose faith in having something real. We can decide it is time to be better and to be around people who know better.

When we are in a healthy relationship, we experience a consistent, safe space to be natural. There is no need to force and fake things. The relationship creates room for us to feel and express the full spectrum of our emotions. If it is anger, then we process that. If it is sadness or great joy, we have room to feel it all. We don't have to hold back because there is room for learning, exploring, and making mistakes. Healthy relationships teach us the respect of mutual boundaries. Friendship reveals multiple passes to stretch them with time and trust. Lovers in authentic relationships transfer power for the sake of flow and unity. The focus is about togetherness, not having an edge over the other.

Sometimes we mistake the dysfunction within our relationships as love. Arguing gets viewed as a sign of passion. Lying gets twisted into a sign of caring. We find ourselves ignoring the red flags that point out problem areas. For the moment, it is easier to stay where it's familiar. But this isn't healthy for our hearts. Dysfunction and denial don't help us heal after disappointment- clarity does. Separating ourselves from negative people and relationships helps recalibrate our minds. With their influence gone we can focus on what's faithful to us. When we break from toxic people, we can see, think, and feel better. We can understand that love is not responsible for mistakes made due to our human nature.

Blaming love for our decisions will not improve our relationships. We have to be accountable for our choices, then learn how to grow from them. We may have had a habit of ignoring intuition before, but now we use it as a guide. We may have chosen to lie to ourselves before, but now we know lies only attract more pain in life. Love exists to add value to our lives and longevity to relationships. Love can improve all things, including behavior, emotion, and habits. Love is not dysfunctional. Love is a powerful step toward peace.

Peace arrives in our hearts after we prepare a place for it. Preparation requires having self-awareness, learning to forgive, and embracing change. Preparing to have a peaceful heart also means clearing out corrupt self-images. In circumstances where our self-esteem is low, we have to clean out shame, guilt, and envy. When we are uncertain about what to do next, we have to remove pride, arrogance, and fear. The biggest thing we can do for peace is change our thoughts - the ones about the past, old flames, and other dead situations. When we start to think in a new way, things in life begin to change for our benefit. We can clear the drama of the past out for peace in the present. This peace creates a place for harmony, calm, and unison. And with peace in our hearts, we can focus on growth and the limitless possibilities ahead.

18. The Old You For The New You

When we begin to process pain, it changes us, and we don't always recognize how. In relationships, many things within a person can shift between the start and the breakup. I have been that person who developed new beliefs, interests, and thought patterns after disappointment. To the unhealed parts of me, the changes meant to stay guarded and closed off. But my healed perspective saw a design for relationships centered on renewal - an exchange of one thing for another. In my case – it was the old me for a new me. Renewal meant exchanging the exhausted feeling I had after knowing breaking up was inevitable for a revitalized spirit, one that could only come from letting go of that relationship.

Renewal is a consistent quality of healthy relationships, and we realize it most with people who inspire us to exchange our misguided ways for better ones. The awakening of self is about exchanging cloudy thoughts of fear to the way of love and possibility. It is switching the way we used to struggle with doubt to the way of confidence and initiative. It is reversing the way we used to hold back from showing our true self to a way of openness and self-assurance. Like pain, people change us, and they influence us to make changes in life. Yes, it hurts, but there is also beauty in the cycle. We get to decide whether any of it makes us a better person. We get the choice of continuing toward the life that we want.

Relationships help increase our discernment. Through them, we can see the difference between someone good for the moment, and one who's good for our lives. Relationships also show us when we're stuck in an unhealthy cycle. We don't always see the self-centeredness, laziness, and bitterness we have inside; however, an intimate relationship can reveal it. Discernment is the way we mentally distinguish the different experiences in life. With it, when something isn't working we can recognize, change, and make adjustments. Our brain can create new patterns that support the way we want to feel, live, and grow. The hurt, shame, doubt, and fear of disappointment can change. In fact, some relationships happen to show us why change is so necessary.

Selfishness, hate, and jealousy are bad habits. They keep us from being happy and they influence negative decision-making. We have a choice not to get depressed and buried by our own negative thoughts and feelings. We can face doubt, understand fear, and still love. We can start today.

Many of our experiences are there to help us with clarity. When we realize the purpose for certain things happening, we can graduate out of the cycles that caused them. There is a reason we do the things that we do, even when we claim to be going with the flow. Reflecting enough to find the reason and seeing the consequence can influence us to adopt healthier habits as we create new cycles in life. When we blame ourselves for something negative, growth is asking - "What can I do differently? How can I create something positive from the lessons my mistakes have taught me?"

Realizing our purpose helps us learn how to create a new self-image, and this is vital for achievement, success, and for making our dreams come true. After we discover a stronger sense of who we are, the goals and vision we believe in must be precise and clear. We have to know and define what we want to achieve for it to happen. We can also bring clarity to a situation by helping people see things that they didn't see before. By clearing up misunderstandings or giving explanations, we grow with those around us.

When trying to get from an old place to a new one, staying focused is integral. A helpful tactic to staying consistent with new changes is tracking the progress. It is encouraging when we can see proof of our work and growth. It feels good to know that we are improving day by day. There are a lot of ways to track our progress without adding unhealthy pressure into our lives. Many people feel more organized with a trusted calendar, journal, or app. These items are good personal support tools. Flipping through the entries on their old pages provides proof that we are not where we once used to be. With experience, we gain the clarity needed to be specific about what we want to achieve. When asked, "Why is it important to you?" We can have an answer because we've been willing to look within. When we break our goals down into steps, it makes our mission of staying focused more manageable. We won't know every detail of the journey, but we do know we will have to change to complete it. We need focus to get things done.

The word, "renewal" is not as glamorous as it sounds. Renewal can be ugly, taxing, and extensive. It won't feel instant. It is going to take some time and a lot of work. We have to be ready to acknowledge our weaknesses and to take note of our setbacks. There will be mistakes and bad choices, but each has something for us to learn. There are always ways to improve the things we do, whether at work, in relationships, and how we treat ourselves. The moments where we fall short are part of the conditioning we need. And they prepare us to become somebody different - a person capable of finding beauty and healing after ugliness and pain.

Accountability is the character trait that helps us stick to our word while we transition and make changes on our journey. We create promises and bonds with friends, family, and our jobs. So sometimes we need a partner who reminds us to be responsible, someone there to make sure we follow through on what is most important to us. We are more likely to complete something if we talk about it to someone else. When we invite nonjudgmental people in as close support, they end up helping us stay centered and balanced. We heal after disappointment by embracing supportive relationships and taking accountability for the changes we know we need to make.

19. Beautiful Amor, Beautiful Us – Babu Spirits

Relationships work in many powerful ways; they influence us to explore, reflect, and grow beyond our comfort zone. Within our relationships, there are spiritual exchanges, revelations, and different levels of connection. Sometimes it is hard to describe how we become close with certain people so fast. It is a welcoming feeling knowing someone who reflects the good parts within us. These relationships aren't always explained or broadcasted, but the comfort is trustworthy. I call these bonds BABU spirits. It is an acronym made to describe feeling safe, valued and connected with someone. Beautiful amour, beautiful us; we have love, and we are love.

Many different spirits enter our lives throughout our journey. Sometimes we discover friendship with a person before we ever knew we needed someone like them. We connect with Babu spirits at different levels of the mind, and we connect with them through many lifetimes and shared lessons. A Babu connection bears light toward our purpose in life. Meeting these people is a signal that we're on the right path. This type of relationship gives us energy, awareness, unconditional love, and compassion. Spiritual connections like these can save our lives. They can help us get to a place of peace, love, and success. Breakdowns, breakthroughs, breakups - it is all so we can grow, through it all we're meant to go forward. Not with our head down, or with our hearts closed, but stronger and with healthy relationships.

Babu spirits are connections that feel like family. We get a strong sense that meeting them isn't a coincidence. With this kind of person, there is a feeling that tells us we've connected with this person for a higher purpose. The connection feels like family, though this type of family is not always related by blood. Sometimes Babu relationships develop through a mutual desire to grow. We stick close to the ones who share our vision for life. We fight for the people who care to help us stand resolute. And we should embrace when it feels right to have trust in them.

Some spiritual connections can only happen after we have learned how to trust because trust creates a sense of confidence. A Babu spirit (Beautiful amour, beautiful us) is someone we believe with surety. We see the authenticity inside their heart and respect the way it shines, no matter how they had to earn it. Their effort to be a better friend could be from losing people in the past, but it taught them to express how they feel. The mistakes and bad choices could be why they move at a slower pace, but at least we know they don't want repeat what they did in the past. We have to appreciate the experiences that make someone recognize when it is time to grow as a person. Spiritual connections happen with individuals who have been in similar situations as us, and they last with people who don't waste time being judgmental because they have had to learn the lesson in the same way.

We can recognize spiritual connections with people when our talents have symmetry. There is a natural sync with our approach to life. We have the same integrity, moral compass, and same grit; we line up, and everything makes sense, it flows. There is no unhealthy competition to be better than them; there is respect and honor for what both people can do well. One of us plays the instrument; the other can sing the lyrics. One of us is there to catch when the other passes. Some people come into our lives without a struggle, and they don't stay to disturb us. They remain to keep our flow going, to be the support we need. People who support themselves tend to offer better support in relationships.

There's nothing like having shared intuition. Knowing you and another person think in similar patterns. With Babu spirits, many times, we are thinking about them right before they contact us. We get visions about them that come true, and they even appear in the few dreams that we remember. In person, we can understand people like this with eye contact and a smile. Sometimes it is a relief when it doesn't always take speaking to communicate in the same room. Our spirit can feel when they need emotional support, and they don't even have to ask. It is a beautiful love. One with symmetry, forward motion, and discovery- it is the kind of love we deserve.

There are people in life who will align with us according to a soul purpose. This could be to support, inspire, and encourage us through our seasons of growth. Others show up to instruct, challenge, and teach us. Sometimes the lesson is to get stronger, other times it is to love better. The point is, we each have a spiritual gift to help one another in life. We meet the people we know for a reason, and we remember them for a purpose.

The Babu spirits teach us to endure our spiritual challenges because they know those experiences help us develop into who we need to be. Discernment, awareness, and a sense of togetherness can come after fighting through the cobwebs of broken relationships. Beyond the tangles of fear and disappointment, we see the people supporting our growth, and we can reach confidently for their love and support. The Babu spirits are there to make sure we feel safe, valued, and connected- they remind us that we are magnificent and that we are loved.

TRUC**E**
Part Five:
EVOLUTION

20. Finding Our Inner Resources

A t our essence, we are spiritual beings traveling through a human experience. The thoughts, feelings, and moods we live moment to moment don't show the total of who we are; they only show pieces. Each one of us has a specific purpose for being alive, something that makes us different from anyone else we know. But as life unfolds and we condition ourselves to flourish, sometimes we can forget how magnificent we are inside. Unresolved and constant disappointment can make us forget about our inner resources. It can make us ignore our spiritual side because we are so caught up in human flaws and life's difficulties. Yet, we grow in consciousness through taking on challenging experiences. This is the heartbreak, the abandonment, and the lack of forgiveness felt at times. It is also the triumph, success, breakthrough, and restoration of our true essence. The spirit within us is creative, intelligent, confident, courageous, and passionate. It is always looking for a way to help us enjoy growing in life.

Resilience is proof of our inner strength. Traumatic experiences like divorce, layoffs, and betrayal change our view of self. Our thoughts have the most impact on our ability to stay resilient. We can start to believe that our mistakes make us less worthy of our desires. In reality, our missteps only help us improve our balance and direction. Even the stumbles teach us how to prevent some future falls from happening. Feeling lost is at times the catalyst a person needs to navigate to a deeper level. It takes a strong person to stay committed to recovery and growth, regardless of what they are hit with. It takes an evolved person to deal with their pain before perpetuating it in someone else's life. We have the strength within us to transform for the better; our spirit desires consistent evolution in life. When we match the spiritual progressiveness inside with a flexible mental attitude, the disappointments of our past lose their sting. With time, we will begin to appreciate what it took to get where we are. And we will know that there is no limit to what we can do next.

In every stage of healing and change, one rule consistently rings true: Whatever we focus on with our thoughts will grow in our lives. Our minds are powerful, and that power is either managed or misused, but never diminished. All around us, change is happening, and we can recognize it more when we are working to do so on the inside. Creativity and intelligence are the cure for feeling stuck and lost. To evolve, we must learn things we didn't think we needed before. The rigid and closed off need to learn compassion and empathy. The strong-willed and assertive need to accept guidance and structure. We have to observe ourselves and our thoughts to learn the places where we can improve. Thinking about what we can do different and then making the changes is how we get new, lasting results.

For every pitfall we face, there is a tool, technique, or approach we can use to overcome it. We don't have to let inexperience force us to feel like victims and screw-ups. In the places we fall short, we can learn to rise. After feeling confused, played, and off balance; we can increase our self-awareness. Trying times teach us how important it is to be versatile in life. The better we know ourselves, the more accurate we become when making adjustments. There are many ways to find success, loving relationships, and symmetry. The most sustainable way is knowing what works best for you. The errors, flaws, and mistakes we make along the way lead us to important tests. They create moments for us to find and address our weaknesses before they cause damage. The pain and disappointment we endure in life teach us how powerful introspection and change can be. Holding on to spite and hate will not welcome anything productive in our hearts. Forgiveness and acceptance are the tools that help us heal, feel love, and move forward in our journey.

As we evolve and heal, love establishes a new formation of thoughts inside us - one that doesn't match negativity, abusive people, or self-sabotage. We create it so that we aren't always at war in our relationships, at work, school, or with family. This new form is about truth, openness, and self-determination. It is a shift in perception, meant to give our life a different set of options. And it is a gift whenever we are able to establish a renewed understanding of the world around us and the spirit within us. The adjustments we make in thoughts and habits help us to recognize and release the things that are bad for us. They show us our capacity to change for the better, even in areas we once thought were impossible.

Some experiences in life happen to influence us into making meaningful choices. With them, we are prompted to do some soul searching to discover our inner resources. These character-defining moments show us our spirit; they help us see our positives. They show the places we excel and traits we thrive with, and they also help us see the dark places within that need light, love, and attention. Uncomfortable breakups, missed opportunities, and losing contact with people happen because sometimes we need to experience what separation feels like to know ourselves in our own right. It is not a form of torture; it is the process of evolution. We need time to see how unique and distinct life is, to explore and learn who we are in the world. Sometimes it hurts, and other times it is so fulfilling that we never want the feeling to end. Through it all, in both the ups and downs, we learn to become all that we are. Everything is happening so that we can learn who we are. When we find trust and use our inner resources, we will make choices that manifest more of what we want in life. And we will stay creative, confident, and courageous on this journey.

21. Soul Growth

The evolution of our soul happens by fully experiencing life. Be it relationships, misfortune, or even fame. When we go through something in life, it is a chance for our soul to expand. Each experience makes us more self-aware and balanced, more equipped to thrive. The soul represents life in its most animate forms. The soul is where we get our senses, desires, affections, and it covers the emotional part of our human nature. Throughout life, we build families, start companies, and create nations. We establish culture, religion, and industry. There is no way to tell how everything will work in the end, but for now, the consequences of those choices are what teach us valuable lessons. And though the lessons vary in many ways, what they all share is a purpose to help us evolve - to ensure that our souls grow.

There are different stages of soul growth. They aren't marked by particular age or time, rather by life experience. Each stage has a distinct focus that requires appropriate learning lessons. When we are infant souls, our primary focus is being alive. Our learning experiences happen through survival, struggle, and awareness of our environment. In this stage, we look at the world from a perspective that says, "This is me, and everything else is separate." We are aware of what we like, a bit of who we are, and how we want things to go. But we tend to be rough around the edges because our personal desires are all that matter to us. Tact and patience are afterthoughts. Instead of thinking before we speak, we say whatever comes to mind. Rather than eye contact and intimacy, we prefer random text and passive communication.

As we journey in life, our infant soul grows into a more developed baby soul, almost toddler-like. At this stage, our focus is belonging to culture, something bigger than self. Through culture, we learn rules, roles, law, and order, along with social awareness. We create a strong sense of identity and an understanding of action and consequence. In this stage, we are more inclined to be judgmental and cruel to people who do not share our same views. Fear and guilt cloud our choices and decision-making. Ultimately, both hurting our relationships and keeping us stuck in a box until we decide to be confident and trust ourselves.

When we begin to trust, we stretch from a baby soul to a stage of youth. The young soul focuses most on being free. In this part of life, we want personal achievements, self-advancement, and independence. We want to know what it is like to do things for ourselves, to love, earn, and live as we want. In our conversations, we want to be the one talking, not the one listening. We want to show our strength, win, and flourish in competition. If it is possible to "get away" with something, young souls are willing to take that chance. When we are in this young stage, appearances are everything, and the issues in the world aren't important, as long as we are free to do what we want. We drive the cool car, date the attractive person, and try to be in the right places. But disappointment teaches us how shortsighted this way of living can be. To be self-determined is one thing, but to be selfish is getting in your own way.

We grow from a young soul to a mature one as we journey through newer experiences. The mature soul is less focused on self and more on coexistence with others. We learn in this stage through interdependence, empathy, and intimacy. It is where we first meet the power of compassion and learn what's needed to improve, heal, and strengthen our relationships. That includes the relationship with self, Spirit, people, work, food, and nature. When we become mature, we look to grow, develop, open doors, and evolve. We may fear being misunderstood, but that does not stop us from showing good will and trust. After disappointment, a mature soul still believes in communication, understanding, purpose, and love.

There are old souls, people who exude a spiritual presence. I am referring to the kind of person who makes eye contact to connect and allows you in. Not for power, or with their ego, but with a fullness of heart. Old souls focus on being part of all-that-is. At this stage, we see individuals as equal pieces of a greater whole. We aren't attached to titles and status; we'd rather be wise counsel, a friend, and a guide. Old souls appreciate symmetry, flow, and the beauty in the entirety of life. They know pain doesn't last, so they don't waste time living in fear. Life isn't meant for us to live afraid.

The people we meet, interests we follow, and places we travel are all to aid in our soul growth. Even when we aren't aware of the reason at the moment, none of this is by accident. Our soul knows we need a combination of life experiences to reach our full capacity. From stage to stage, there is no clock, only choices, and lessons to learn. Everything has a cycle, and we are always changing. As we evolve, that cycle will be what brings us together instead of pushing us further apart. The turning points, stepping-stones, and relationships are soul-growing experiences. The more developed we are in soul, the better our relationships are in life.

22. The Second Half

The first half of life is preparing us for whatever we will need to do or be in the second half. We can look at the events, relationships, and defining moments as set-ups for a bigger reason. Each living soul has a life path at birth. It represents who we are and the native traits we carry throughout life. The first half is for discovery, exploring, and strengthening. The second half is how we live after we realize what we were born to contribute to the world. Our paths will often include a particular task, one that has a greater purpose than we know in our early stages. This life work will usually become the primary focus of our journey as our souls evolve. It is what is meant when we talk about finding our purpose.

When we are aware and prepared for our purpose, we can navigate the twists and turns of life with grace. We don't have to look back in worry, in fear of change; we don't have to dread what's ahead of us. In fact, we can release emotional baggage, stress, and uncertainty altogether. Letting go of the past allows us to focus on here and now. It helps us choose more empowering thoughts than the ones that say, "People don't change" and "Love always hurts." It is a chance to free our mind from negativity. No more running from thoughts about an ex, or getting goosebumps at the mention of a painful memory. The past is over. Healing is not a desire to change the first part of our life. It is an acceptance that there is still some growing left for us to do in the second.

We connect with people in many ways throughout our evolution. Mental, physical, emotional, and spiritual connections all stimulate different areas of our growth. The mental connections make sure we grow in intellect. We're enlightened through conversations that share what we've felt, experienced, and learned. The physical connections awaken our senses to the touch, voice, taste, and feel of life. Through them, we experience love, sorrow, joy, remorse, bliss, and pain. Emotional connections increase our sense of community; we attract people to us by being empathetic and showing that we understand. The spiritual connections keep us balanced, poised, and in a composed nature. They remind us that all good things come together for our benefit in the end. The active connections we make help us renew and bond the good from the first half of life into the second.

We all can help each other evolve beyond the pain and disappointing moments. It starts with creating a culture of fellowship. Healed people heal people. They take the good that life has taught them and use it to help others mend relationships, grow, and love. At first, it may not seem reasonable to talk about feelings, fear, or aspirations with people who are not in our inner circle. But the perspective from someone on the outside could help us see things that we couldn't see by being so close. In fellowship with like-minded people, we are heard, received, and affirmed in positive ways. When we talk about our dreams and career changes, healthy association says, "Be bold and go after it." When we're losing confidence, and aiming too low, healthy fellowship reminds us to "Stop settling." It reminds us to be who God designed us to be, and that is loving, encouraging, and whole.

Everything we endure has a purpose and helps us develop the personality we need to be productive in life. For example, life prepared the ones who have felt emotions of abandonment to work in areas that help restore family. It prepared the ones who have felt tough love and rejection to be supportive, giving, and dependable citizens in their community. The experiences in our lives make their impact to teach us the vital things we need to know about ourselves, and the things we need to continue evolving. When we implement knowledge, love, and compassion into our personality, we are always going to have the right people around us in the end.

With every breath, there is an opportunity for our soul's progression. If we settle for the mindset that nothing can change, then nothing will. The second half of life is about opening up in heart, mind, and spirit for evolution. People want to see us bounce back from our shortcomings and get stronger; they want to know it is possible. And beyond that, we deserve to see ourselves as whole, loveable, and worthy of good relationships.

Disappointment is going to happen, but don't ever use it as an excuse to give up on love. Right now, decide you are going to be someone who keeps the faith. Decide that you will trust yourself and that you have the resolve to heal and love again. Be patient with the process; you don't have to rush or try to force anything, life is unfolding the way it needs to. Understand and appreciate where you are, what you've been through, and the blessings that are ahead. As you gain clarity about what works for you, allow yourself to evolve and blossom. Allow yourself to be bold, confident, free, and at peace. The love and relationships that you deserve are on its way, leave the past where it was and keep your heart open to the future.

Other Titles
by Rob Hill Sr.

*FOR SINGLE PEOPLE WHO STILL UNDERSTAND
THE VALUE OF RELATIONSHIPS

*I GOT YOU

*ABOUT SOMETHING REAL

*THE MISSING PIECE
(COMING SPRING/SUMMER 2018)

Website: robhillsr.com
Instagram: robhillsr
Twitter: @RobHillSr
Facebook: RobHillSr
SoundCloud: https://soundcloud.com/robhillsr
YouTube: https://www.youtube.com/user/RobHillSr

Made in the USA
Middletown, DE
15 November 2017